BOY SCOUTS OF AMERICA
MERIT BADGE SERIES

VETERINARY MEDICINE

"Enhancing our youths' competitive edge through merit badges"

BOY SCOUTS OF AMERICA®

Requirements

1. Discuss with your counselor the roles a veterinarian plays in the following:

   a. Companion or small animal medicine, and equine medicine

   b. Food animal or large animal medicine

   c. Exotic animal medicine

   d. Marine animal medicine (mammal and fish)

   e. Poultry medicine

   f. Wildlife medicine and aquaculture medicine

2. Discuss with your counselor the roles a veterinarian plays in the following:

   a. Public health medicine and zoonotic disease surveillance and control

   b. The military

   c. Food safety and inspection

   d. Laboratory animal medicine and research

   e. Teaching and government

3. Describe the training required to become a veterinarian. Where is the veterinary medical college nearest you? Describe the prerequisites for applying to veterinary school.

35962
ISBN 978-0-8395-5004-4
©2012 Boy Scouts of America
2014 Printing

4. Tell your counselor what a registered veterinary technician (R.V.T.) or animal health technician (A.H.T.) is. Describe the training required to become an R.V.T. or A.H.T. Where is the school or facility for R.V.T. or A.H.T. training nearest you? Describe the role an R.V.T. or A.H.T. would play in assisting a veterinarian working in three of the practice types listed in requirement 1.

5. Discuss with your merit badge counselor the role a veterinarian plays in the human-animal bond.

6. Do ONE of the following:

    a. Visit a veterinary clinic, hospital, or veterinary referral teaching hospital that does work in one of the practices listed in requirement 1. Spend as much time as you can observing the veterinarians and their staff. Write a report on what you observed and learned at the facility. Share your report with your counselor.

    b. Spend as much time as possible with a veterinarian who works in one of the fields listed in requirement 2. Learn what special training beyond veterinary medical school may have been required for that position. Learn about any special or unusual activities required of this position. Write a report on what you have learned about this field of veterinary medicine. Include in your report how this field serves the needs of the general public. Share your report with your counselor.

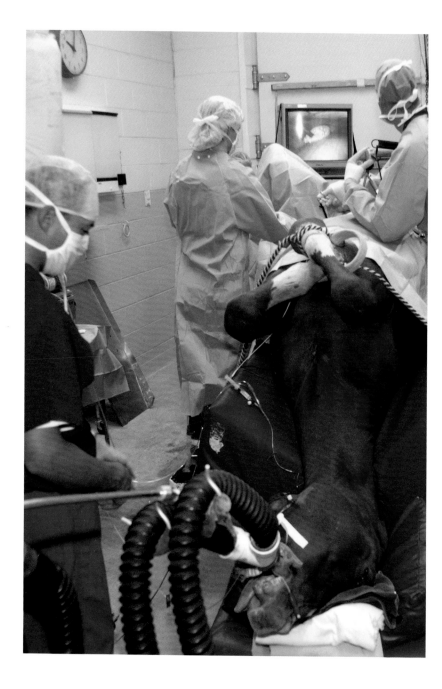

Contents

Introduction

Doctors of veterinary medicine are trained medical professionals whose primary responsibility is to ensure and protect the health and welfare of animals and people. The high-tech world of today's veterinary medicine, with its futuristic diagnostic machines and state-of-the-art hospital facilities, is a product of the long history of contact between humans and animals.

The earliest evidence of veterinary medicine can be traced to the ancient Egyptians. For as long as humans have kept domesticated animals, first as beasts of burden and then as companions, a human-animal bond has existed between people and animals. With that bond came a responsibility to nurture the well-being of animals by keeping them healthy and curing the many disease problems associated with human-animal contact.

The earliest efforts to improve the quality of life of domesticated animals probably involved nothing more than improving basic animal husbandry practices. Better feed and shelter improved the animals' chances of living through another winter and producing more offspring. Later, attention to hoof needs decreased lameness and lengthened the working life of hooved animals. The practice also gave rise to the *farrier*, or horseshoer. When breeding sporting and hunting dogs and horses became popular, commitment to the well-being of these animals became commonplace.

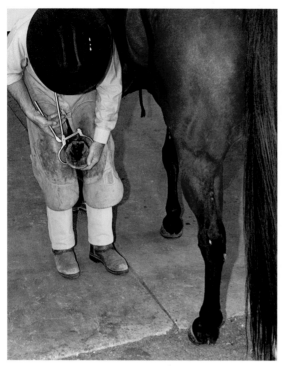

A farrier, or horseshoer, in action

From the 1700s to the early 1900s, as wars in Europe and America relied more heavily on horses and other livestock to move vast armies, the need to care for those animals became more important. By the 1800s in North America, special schools had been established to teach people how to care for animals. By 1920, there were 14 veterinary schools in the United States, and by 1960, the number had grown to 19. Today, there are 28 veterinary schools in the United States, with more being planned for the future.

Until the 1930s, a veterinarian driving from farm to farm in a pickup truck provided most veterinary medical services. In those days, before the discovery of antibiotics, we saw a different type of animal health care than we witness today. Beginning in the 1950s, when house pets became more common, the science of veterinary medicine began to develop in leaps and bounds. Today, it is estimated that the knowledge and technology of the veterinary profession doubles every 24 to 36 months. Currently, more than 67,000 veterinarians work in the United States.

The field of veterinary medicine in the 21st century is one of the most exciting medical professions. The skills of a veterinarian are practiced with cutting-edge technology and treatment options, and the profession offers a wide range of career choices. Through their work, veterinarians also have the opportunity to contribute to the health of the community and the nation.

As you explore the world of veterinary medicine while working on this merit badge, keep in mind that the long-term goal of becoming a veterinarian starts with your successes today. It also is helpful to have an open and curious mind. But most important, you must care about animals and have a cheerful and understanding nature toward people.

Now, let's learn more about veterinarians and veterinary medicine.

Veterinary Specialists

This chapter explores a wide variety of veterinary specialties.

Because of the highly skilled scientific training they receive in veterinary medical school, veterinarians are regarded as well-qualified scientists capable of working in a number of fields. As a result, veterinarians enjoy a wide variety of career choices. In addition to practicing animal medicine, veterinarians have been members of Congress, governors, directors of government agencies and private organizations, consultants on research projects, and even astronauts. Veterinarians also serve as consultants to other veterinarians for medical and business matters, and they serve as administrators for the many veterinary associations within the profession.

Veterinarian's Oath

Being admitted to the profession of veterinary medicine, I solemnly swear to use my scientific knowledge and skills for the benefit of society through the protection of animal health, the relief of animal suffering, the conservation of animal resources, the promotion of public health, and the advancement of medical knowledge.

I will practice my profession conscientiously, with dignity, and in keeping with the principles of veterinary medical ethics.

I accept as a lifelong obligation the continual improvement of my professional knowledge and competence.

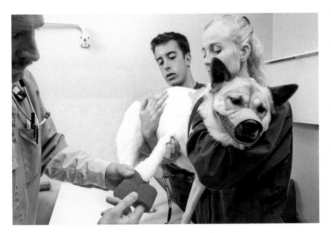

Companion Animal Veterinarians

If you had asked people 50 years ago what veterinarians do, they likely would have answered that a veterinarian is a doctor who treats horses and farm animals such as cattle, sheep, and hogs. Today, however, when most people think of a veterinarian they imagine a doctor who treats companion animals like dogs and cats. Companion animal practice, also called small animal practice, is the branch of veterinary medicine that deals with dogs and cats kept as pets.

Since World War II, Americans have become more affluent and our pets have become more like family members. As a result, veterinarians are expected to provide state-of-the-art medical and surgical procedures and services for our pets. Today, a modern companion animal hospital contains equipment, medicine, and supplies that are more sophisticated than those available to human hospitals only a few years ago. Sophisticated equipment, such as ultrasound machines and laser surgery units, often is commonplace. Some veterinary facilities even have CAT scan and MRI capabilities, while some major referral facilities can provide kidney transplants and heart bypass surgeries.

The daily routine of a companion animal veterinarian is varied and challenging, which provides the fun and excitement of this area of veterinary medicine. No two days are the same. In a given day, a veterinarian might rotate from being a surgeon (fixing a fractured leg), to being an internist (doing an electrocardiogram [EKG] on a dog's failing heart), an obstetrician

As strange as it might seem, all domestic dogs, from the very small Chihuahua to the massive Saint Bernard, all belong to the same species, *Canis familiaris.* Likewise, all domestic cats, from the dignified Siamese to the homeless alley cat, all belong to the species *Felis catus.*

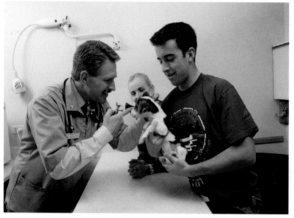

(delivering a litter of puppies), a behavioral psychiatrist (helping psychologically challenged pets), a nutritionist, or even a grief counselor. In addition, a companion animal veterinarian must shift gears to provide these services to completely different species, as well as the young and old and the large and small.

Another important aspect of companion animal practice is preventive medicine. Just as people take precautions against catching diseases, companion animal veterinarians provide vaccinations, medicines, and surgical procedures to prevent diseases and other problems from affecting the quality of life of our pets. It is far safer, less painful, and less expensive to prevent a disease than to try to cure it after it has occurred. Companion animal veterinarians also devote a lot of time to educating pet owners about the importance of preventive health care.

For many veterinarians, companion animal practice offers a great opportunity to engage in sophisticated medicine in comfortable conditions and with reasonable time off and a decent income. A companion animal veterinarian might own and operate a clinic or might work with a team of veterinarians in a hospital. Companion animal veterinarians are vital members of their community's health-care system. Additionally, they are a vital link in the human-animal bond, which all pet owners cherish. Because of the many different health-care roles that veterinarians fill, they generally are well-respected within their community.

The educational requirements for a companion animal veterinarian are essentially the same as for other areas of the profession. Also, due to pet owners' demand for sophisticated medicine and surgery, there is the additional opportunity, through further study, to become a specialist with a concentration in treating a particular species (cats only, for example) or a specific aspect of medical care (such as diagnostics).

For veterinarians in general and the companion animal practitioner specifically, few vocations offer more challenge, more diversity, or more opportunity for dedication to public service—not only to animals, but the pet-loving public as well.

Equine Veterinarians

Historically, the field of equine (horse) veterinary medicine was limited to taking care of draft horses, "cowponies," cavalry mounts, and mules. In the early 1900s, there were about 27 million horses in these categories in the United States. Today, working with an equine population of about 4 million, the field of equine veterinary medicine uses technologically advanced forms of medical and surgical care, including preventive care, nutrition, conditioning and breeding soundness, housing, and transportation.

Equine veterinarians might treat the "backyard" pony or pleasure horse, cattle horses, rodeo horses, or parade or ceremonial horses belonging to the military.

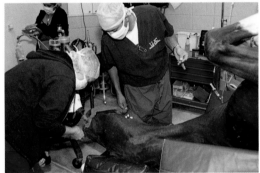

Equine veterinarians enjoy great variety in their day-to-day work.

Specialized vehicle used by equine veterinarians

There also are backcountry packhorses and mules, donkeys and burros, show horses (Lipizzan stallions, Clydesdale parade teams), racehorses, breeding horses, circus and zoo equines (even zebras), large draft horses, and miniature horse breeds.

Equine veterinarians work in a variety of settings. Imagine traveling to a ranch or farm to examine a workhorse. A visit to a thoroughbred racing stable or a racetrack might be another workplace. The local circus or zoo might ask you to examine some of its animals. Because many people own horses for riding, a house call to a suburban home might be a common work site. Equine veterinarians also work in state-of-the-art equine hospitals and teaching facilities. At these institutions, CAT scans, MRIs, and sophisticated surgical procedures are performed. Some equine veterinarians travel with the military or peace corps to provide services in countries where horses are still a major source of livelihood, much as they were in our country a century ago.

Veterinary medicine has many areas of specialization. After completing veterinary medical school, a veterinarian may pursue advanced training in more than 30 different specialty fields. Completing the required advanced training and passing a very comprehensive examination in the chosen area gives a veterinarian "diplomat" status in that field as recognized by the American Veterinary Medical Association.

Some examples of the many AVMA-recognized specialty areas include toxicology, laboratory medicine, theriogenology (reproduction), anesthesiology, clinical pharmacology, behavior, dermatology, cardiology, neurology, oncology (cancer), microbiology, ophthalmology (eyes), pathology (anatomic, clinical), preventive medicine, epidemiology, radiation oncology, surgery, and equine, bovine, poultry, canine, feline, porcine, and zoological medicine.

Equine veterinarians need many tools and skills, one of the most important being the ability to work well with people. The types of tools used depend on the type of medical service the veterinarian provides. In general these tools are expensive and large. Thus, many equine veterinarians have specially built vehicles for traveling to farms and horse facilities for onsite service. Also, due to the size and weight of their patients, many equine veterinarians work with veterinary assistants.

As with all the veterinary fields, training to become an equine veterinarian begins with a high school education followed by a strong college education and graduation from a veterinary medical school. Beyond doctorate of veterinary medicine (D.V.M. or V.M.D.), some equine veterinarians seek specialized training to become board-certified specialists in equine medicine or related fields.

Large Animal Veterinarians

Think about the different types of meat we eat and their origin. Hamburgers, steaks, and roasts come from cattle and even buffalo (bovine). Bacon, sausage, ham, and barbecued pork ribs come from pigs (porcine), and lamb chops come from sheep (ovine). Now, think of the many dairy products we consume. These mainly come from cattle and sometimes goats. Some of the exotic pack animals, like llamas, do a number of

things for us. All of these animals, whether raised individually or in large herds, must be healthy and free of diseases. Ensuring the health of these animals is the responsibility of the large animal, or food animal, veterinarian.

Historically, most food animals in the United States were raised in small groups on small plots of land for use by a single family. As the country's population grew, small farms could not meet the

Where do large animal veterinarians work? One place might be a feedlot. Feedlots, which are densely populated animal-raising facilities, might have an on-site veterinarian. Some of the largest feedlot operations have veterinarians who fly from feedlot to feedlot to cover all the herds.

nation's demand for meat and dairy products. Subsequently, larger production methods, such as cattle and sheep ranches, developed. More recently, when range land became scarcer and the cost of raising livestock became more competitive, range herds gave way to feedlots. The same changes occurred in the dairy industry. Today, many dairy operations are so large that herds of milk cows are milked in rotation 24 hours a day.

Large animal veterinarians work in a variety of places. Every state in the United States produces livestock. From the vastness of the open ranges in many western states to the densely populated eastern seaboard states, large animal veterinarians are called upon to ensure the health of our food-producing animals. This challenge for the large animal veterinarian helps guarantee the safety and quality of our nation's food supply.

Some areas well-suited to raising one type of animal, such as pigs (swine), might have dozens of veterinarians servicing numerous swine producers. In some areas, where cows, sheep, and pigs are raised on small parcels of land, large animal veterinarians might make house calls or the veterinarian might provide service from a hospital designed for larger animals. Some large animal veterinarians teach at universities while also tending livestock kept for teaching purposes.

Large animal veterinarians in the dairy industry help manage animal health and also work closely with the dairy producer to manage the herd's breeding program and the dairy's milking technology.

A large animal veterinarian uses a wide variety of equipment and instruments. A vehicle specially adapted for large animal veterinary work is a standard tool. They also use specialized medicines, instruments, and restraint devices.

Whatever the location or the type of animal being treated, the large animal veterinarian is guaranteed variety. With the number of different animals and the assortment of health problems each animal could have, it is easy to imagine that no two days would be the same. The satisfaction of working

Large animal veterinarians are the first line of defense against diseases that can harm our nation's food supply and the health of our citizens. Countless exotic, or foreign, diseases can affect large animals, and subsequently, people. Fortunately, our nation's livestock populations are largely free from these diseases. However, because their exposure to such diseases is largely absent, our livestock populations are susceptible to catching foreign diseases.

outdoors with hard-working ranchers and livestock producers makes this an especially enjoyable area of veterinary medicine. The work is more physical than other fields, but it is full of rewards and challenges.

Training to become a food animal or large animal veterinarian begins with a good high school education followed by a strong college education and graduation from veterinary medical school. Beyond the doctor of veterinary medicine degree (D.V.M. or V.M.D.), some food animal or large animal veterinarians seek specialized training to become board-certified specialists in large animal medicine or related fields.

Exotic Animal Veterinarians

A typical day for an exotic animal veterinarian might start with a turtle that cannot open its eyes, followed by a boa constrictor

The work of some large animal veterinarians takes them to extraordinary places. For example, large animal veterinarians might work with the circus. Or, they might work in other countries, where water buffalo, elephants, camels, llamas, and other animals are as vital to the quality of life as a car, truck, or tractor is to us.

The turtle is considered an exotic animal.

Prairie dog

Guinea pig

Arizona tiger salamander

that will not eat, a jungle cat that has swallowed a ball too large to pass, an Indonesian parrot trying but unable to lay an egg, and, finally, a ferret with the flu. These are just some of the problems likely to be seen in the busy schedule of an exotic animal veterinarian.

Exotic animals are animals that are not native to the place they are found. However, in the veterinary profession, wildlife and small caged animals like hamsters, gerbils, ferrets, and reptiles are considered exotic animals, too. Additionally, exotic animal veterinarians might treat wild animals, which are not recommended as pets.

Exotic animals have many different physical and nutritional needs and can develop a multitude of unusual diseases. It's what makes this practice extra challenging. Only in the past 20 or so years has there been much advancement in the field, in particular the medical and surgical care of exotic species. Thanks to exotic animal veterinarians, their research partners, and modern scientific techniques, the health care and welfare of exotic animals has substantially improved in recent years.

Exotic animal veterinarians often work in private practice, where they have special equipment, medications, and cages for various exotic animals. Exotic animal veterinarians also work for zoos, circuses, or wild animal parks.

The educational requirements for exotic animal medicine are the same as for other types of veterinary medicine. However,

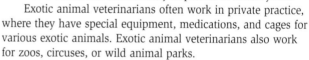

Exotic animal veterinarians might also aid wildlife affected by natural disasters, such as wildfires and floods, and industrial accidents, such as an oil spill. Exotic animal veterinarians also help monitor the numerous zoonotic diseases (diseases that can infect both people and animals) that might be carried into the United States by animals from other countries.

Sumatran rhino

a strong background in vertebrate zoology and postgraduate training in exotic animal medicine is highly recommended for this field.

> All exotic animal veterinarians respect the wildness of their patients. Most veterinarians would not recommend exotic animals as pets. However, if an exotic pet is presented for care, the exotic animal veterinarian is the best-trained person for the task.

Marine Animal Veterinarians

What comes to mind when you think of a doctor who treats whales, dolphins, great white sharks, and other marine animals? Undoubtedly, excitement, adventure, and danger pop into your mind. Perhaps you imagine being part of the crew that conducts research off the coast of Hawaii or Alaska or in the Caribbean.

Marine animal veterinarians deal with the mammals, fish, and reptiles of the sea. Though marine animal veterinarians treat a fewer number of species than other veterinarians, the diversity of marine animals and marine animal habitats offers unique challenges. The main challenge is the environment

in which marine animals live: the sea. Water quality, environmental pollution, global influences on ocean warming, red tides (a poisonous condition made by the sudden overgrowth of algae), and overfishing (which disrupts the balance of the ocean's food chain) all affect the conditions that a marine animal veterinarian might encounter. In addition, marine animal veterinarians must understand and consider the large physical differences between species.

Marine animal veterinarians often work with endangered and protected species. Many wildlife experts, marine biologists, and regulatory agents are involved with these marine animals. However, only the veterinarian has the expertise to address the medical needs of animals.

Marine animal medicine is a fairly young practice within veterinary medicine. Although the knowledge base of the practice grows each year, much research into the medicine and disease of marine animals is needed. Although the field for employment is small, tremendous opportunities exist for veterinarians who wish to enter it. Zoos and aquariums, government and military agencies, universities and research institutions, conservation organizations, and private industries all offer

Did you know that the U.S. Navy uses certain marine animals as part of its underwater surveillance program? Small underwater cameras can be attached to the fins of specially trained dolphins to help detect mines and other underwater hazards. These animals are valuable, and it is the marine animal veterinarian's task to help keep them healthy.

opportunities to veterinarians with a serious interest in marine animal medicine.

Educational requirements for marine animal veterinary medicine include a doctorate of veterinary medicine and a strong background in all types of biology, with a special emphasis on marine biology.

Poultry Veterinarians

What do you think about when you hear the word "poultry"? Chickens and turkeys might come to mind. While this is correct, the term "poultry" and the arena of poultry veterinary medicine include more than just chickens and turkeys.

Poultry veterinary medicine is different than most areas of science. Instead of working one-on-one with an individual animal, the poultry veterinarian generally works with very large flocks containing thousands of birds. The poultry industry, in which the poultry veterinarian works, deals with millions of animals at any one time.

The production and disease management of chickens and turkeys are the two biggest areas of involvement for poultry veterinarians.

The White Leghorn is a champion egg-layer.

However, poultry veterinarians also treat other species of birds, such as ducks, geese, and ratites (ostriches and emus) that are raised for meat, plumage, and eggs. Additionally, poultry veterinarians provide care to birds at zoo aviaries or special institutions involved in the care of endangered species of wild birds, such as the majestic California condor.

Very large production companies own most of the poultry raised in the United States, and they employ the largest number of poultry veterinarians. Veterinarians who work for these large companies help manage the health of the entire flock as well as ensure the safety of our country's food supply. These

Emus

Poultry veterinarians and poultry veterinary food inspectors serve as our country's first line of defense against foreign diseases that could destroy the entire poultry industry.

veterinarians also play an important public health role in the prevention and control of human food-borne illnesses associated with poultry, such as salmonella poisoning.

Some poultry veterinarians work for pharmaceutical (drug) companies that develop vaccines for all species of poultry. These veterinarians also help monitor the chemical residues and toxins in poultry products. Other poultry veterinarians work for the U.S. Department of Agriculture in research or at diagnostic labs where the detection of foreign diseases is monitored.

Other poultry veterinarians work with ostriches and emus. In other parts of the world, these large flightless birds are considered a major source of food. Recently, they have become popular in the United States as a food source, too.

The poultry industry is a multibillion-dollar industry in the United States. When you consider that over 50 million chickens and 1 billion eggs are produced each week in the United States, one can see how important the poultry veterinarian's work is to our economy and the world food market.

Training to become a poultry veterinarian begins with a good high school education followed by a strong college education and graduation from a veterinary medical school. Beyond a doctorate in veterinary medicine, the field requires advanced study in poultry medicine and related fields.

Wildlife Veterinarians

It is Sunday morning; you have just finished breakfast when the telephone rings. The state game protector (wildlife officer) for your area asks if you could accompany her to a farm some distance away. A farmer has reported that a large number of blue jays and crows are sick and dying on his farm and on other farms in the area. He notes that the mosquitoes have been particularly bad for several weeks, due to all the rain.

The wildlife officer asks if you have any idea what might cause such a problem. She called you because she knows that you, as a wildlife veterinarian, are an expert on the diseases of birds and wild animals. You suspect West Nile Virus, but you need to confirm the diagnosis. You agree to accompany the wildlife officer to the farm.

Wildlife veterinarians face many situations similar to the one described above. West Nile Virus in birds and other animals, Wasting disease in deer, accidental poisonings from chemical contamination, and rabies control in woodland mammals (such as raccoons, foxes, and skunks) are a few of the problems encountered routinely.

The USDA is responsible for preventing foreign diseases from entering the United States. Wildlife veterinarians serve as part of the team that protects our country from the foreign diseases that exotic species might carry.

Human health also is a concern because many of the diseases that affect wildlife can be transmitted to humans (zoonotic diseases).

Due to the many diseases that affect wildlife, nearly all state wildlife agencies use the expertise of wildlife veterinarians as part of the effort to keep wildlife populations as healthy as possible and to reduce the risk of transmitting diseases to humans.

Opportunities for wildlife veterinarians are not as numerous as for other veterinarians, but positions are available in all parts of the country. Special training beyond a doctorate in veterinary medicine is necessary to practice wildlife medicine. Some colleges of veterinary medicine have special postgraduate training in wildlife medicine.

Aquaculture Veterinarians

The role of the veterinarian in aquaculture (fish and shellfish farming) is gaining recognition. Recreational fisheries, commercial producers of fish, large aquariums such as Sea World, and pet and hobby fish enthusiasts have created a growing demand for veterinary services.

Aquaculture medicine uses the principles of veterinary medicine to maintain healthy colonies of fish and other aquatic animals. This field of veterinary medicine is distinct from other areas of aquatic science, such as marine biology. As the world population grows, aquaculture will help provide an adequate food supply, and the work of aquaculture veterinarians will be critical to the industry's success.

Students interested in aquaculture medicine must earn a doctorate in veterinary medicine. Postgraduate training in aquaculture medicine is offered at some schools of veterinary medicine. Many opportunities, especially in the coming years, await individuals trained in aquaculture medicine.

Public Health Veterinarians

You might not hear much about public health veterinarians because most of them work for local, state, and federal agencies. Veterinarians who work in public health are the silent sentinels protecting America's public health and our quality of life.

Public health veterinarians work in a number of areas of national and public concern. For example, they are involved in matters related to terrorism and the use of disease agents for biological warfare, such as anthrax and botulism. Also, public health veterinarians monitor and prevent zoonotic diseases that are spread by insects, such as Lyme's disease, Rocky Mountain spotted fever, and West Nile Virus, and other diseases, such as rabies, influenza, HIV, and plague.

Public health veterinarians also monitor water and food supplies and inspect most of the meat and egg products consumed in the United States.

The professional life of a public health veterinarian is varied and exciting. Being a trained doctor and also part detective, part researcher, part public servant, and part watchdog for the nation's health is what being a public health veterinarian is all about.

Governmental agencies that work with public health veterinarians include the Centers for Disease Control and Prevention, the Environmental Protection Agency, the Food and Drug Administration, the U.S. Department of Agriculture, state and federal fish and wildlife agencies, and local public health departments. Additionally, public health veterinarians may work for the U.S. Public Health Service on American Indian reservations, in the military, or at the National Institutes of Health.

Public health veterinarians have monitored the potential for zoonotic disease problems for the Boy Scouts of America. Working with other public health specialists, these veterinarians have helped identify and solve public health issues before world and national jamborees. Public health veterinarians also have helped find ways to reduce contact between wildlife and humans at Philmont Scout Ranch.

Every veterinarian has a federal and state requirement to keep a look out for and report zoonotic diseases.

Military Veterinarians

In the early days of our nation's military, when soldiers rode horses, farriers accompanied the military on the frontier. These individuals cared for the Army's horses, mules, and other livestock. In 1910, after the Spanish-American War, Congress established the U.S. Army Veterinary Corps to inspect all animals and animal products used by the military and other governmental services.

During World War I, veterinarians performed a lot of trauma surgery on horses in battle. When Congress learned that veterinarians were far better at trauma surgery than physicians, Congress decreed that veterinarians be the first professionals mobilized—before dentists and other health-care providers—to assist physicians in performing trauma surgery on injured soldiers.

Over the years, military working dogs have played an important role in military functions. They have been trained as attack dogs and sentries, for tracking and rescue, and to detect explosives and narcotics. Each of these highly trained dogs is worth several thousand of dollars, and military veterinarians are their sole health-care providers on and off the battlefield.

When gas-powered vehicles replaced horses after World War I, many thought it signaled the end of veterinary practice in the military as well as the public sector. However, because veterinarians were still required to inspect food, they continued to be a part of the military. By the end of World War II, veterinarians were inspecting all civilian industries seeking to sell food to the military.

After World War II, veterinarians served in the U.S. Air Force and provided the same services that U.S. Army veterinarians did. In 1981, Congress decided that U.S. Air Force veterinarians would manage communicable disease control programs, while the U.S. Army veterinarians would continue their traditional roles. Today, U.S. Army veterinarians also provide services to the U.S. Navy and U.S. Marine Corps.

Today, U.S. Army veterinarians are stationed around the world. They provide animal health care, monitor public and environmental health, and inspect and obtain food. Veterinary officers serve as members of special forces units, as instructors at military training schools, and in all specialties of veterinary medicine within the military system. Military veterinarians also play a part in helping countries rebuild after wars or other national disasters.

In addition to having a doctorate in veterinary medicine, military veterinarians are commissioned officers in the U.S. military and undergo special training to prepare them for military assignments.

Food Safety and Inspection Veterinarians

It is easy to take for granted the inspection and safety monitoring of our food supplies. However, food-borne diseases such as salmonella, E. coli, staphylococcus, pork trichina, tuberculosis, and many others would be commonplace without food safety inspections.

Food safety and inspection begins well before any food item arrives at your local grocery store. Fresh meats, for example, are inspected numerous times between the slaughterhouse and the delivery truck. Fresh eggs and milk undergo similar inspections for quality and wholesomeness. Even fruits, vegetables, and nuts are inspected.

Who inspects all these food products and helps guarantee the safety of our food supply? Veterinarians, along with legions of veterinary science technicians. Why? Because veterinarians have the training in animal health and disease to recognize which animal products are safe to be eaten, and which are not. They understand the requirements for the proper handling, storage, and processing of food products. They also are trained to recognize the presence of foreign diseases found in food products that were processed in other countries.

Because the USDA handles food safety and inspection, most veterinarians working in this field are employed by the government. Food safety and inspection assignments also fall on the shoulders of military veterinarians, who make sure that all the food provided to troops—overseas and stateside—is wholesome and safe.

Food safety and inspection veterinarians work in slaughterhouses, packing plants, cold-storage facilities, receiving stations, food manufacturing plants, food-testing and toxicology laboratories, and any other sites where food products are processed.

To practice food safety and inspection, a veterinarian with a doctorate in veterinary medicine must also have training in food inspection techniques and USDA health standards.

Laboratory Animal Medicine and Research Veterinarians

Laboratory animal medicine and research veterinary medicine have much in common. Both fields apply the skills learned in veterinary school to a number of areas of study. Also, rather than working in a practice setting, veterinarians in these specialties usually work or teach at a college, university, pharmaceutical company, government facility, or independent laboratory.

A veterinarian working in laboratory animal medicine provides medical care for animals used in research. This means performing surgery, treating diseases, and monitoring the behavior of animals such as mice, rats, guinea pigs, hamsters, rabbits, dogs, monkeys, cattle, sheep, goats, fish, amphibians, and various species of birds.

To do all of these different tasks, laboratory animal veterinarians must have specialized knowledge of surgery, physiology, and toxicology (the science of dealing with the effects, antidotes, and detection of poisons) in the laboratory animals with which they work. The veterinarian sometimes is a member of the research team and helps design studies, interpret results, and publish articles about the research in scientific journals. Of course, the humane and respectful care and treatment of all animals is a major responsibility of everyone doing experiments on animals, and the veterinarian usually takes the lead role.

Research veterinarians investigate new medicines, biotechnical and diagnostic tests, food technologies, and other new technologies. Research veterinarians might also investigate the exotic and infectious diseases that threaten public health. Or, research veterinarians might work in the emerging field of genetic research.

Laboratory animal medicine and research veterinarians usually work on a team of scientists, much like an individual Scout works with his patrol. This means that people skills are very important in these fields. Working as a team means sharing the workload and using good communication skills to share information. Good teamwork might help solve the mysteries of a disease, for example.

To practice laboratory animal medicine or to conduct research, veterinarians must have a doctorate in veterinary medicine and possibly special training in laboratory animal diseases, anatomy, physiology, and statistics. These special training requirements call for one to five years of additional course work. A solid foundation in math and science, starting at the level of school in which you are now, will be helpful.

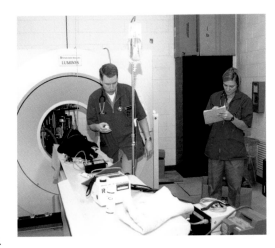

Teaching Veterinarians

Many exciting and rewarding opportunities exist for veterinarians who become educators. In most cases, teachers of veterinary medicine have advanced training beyond the doctorate of veterinary medicine that qualifies them to train students in any number of subjects. Some of the specialty fields at the forefront of veterinary education are molecular biology, biotechnology, environmental toxicology, nanotechnology, public health, and infectious diseases.

Most educators at the level of these specialty fields teach at a school of veterinary medicine or at a university or college. As an educator, your career would be challenging and diverse, with a mixture of classroom instruction, research, and clinical instruction.

Strong technical skills and the ability to work well with people are prime requirements for working in veterinary medicine.

An advantage of teaching at a university is having access to the high-tech tools of medical research, such as an atomic force microscope, gamma spectrometer, and PET scanner. These tools are very expensive and are rarely found outside of a university setting. Another advantage is the potential to work with well-regarded experts in the field of veterinary medicine.

What subjects do you think you would like to teach? Anatomy, biochemistry, surgery, pathology, genetics, and clinical services are just a few of the many subjects that veterinary students must master. Added to the challenge of teaching is the enjoyment of stimulating contact with students.

Most educators also conduct research on the topic area in which they are most interested. While much of the satisfaction of teaching comes from working with and advising students, a great deal of professional reward comes from contributing to science through research. Imagine that your research efforts helped uncover a new disease and then a treatment for that disease. This type of opportunity, offered to the veterinary teacher, could be the achievement of a lifetime.

While the economic forecast for educators is quite good, their salaries are governed by individual schools and might be lower than income made in private practice. However, professors usually receive many benefits, including vacation schedules and retirement plans. Together, the salary and benefits make this area of veterinary medicine very appealing.

Government Veterinarians

Veterinarians work for the government at federal, state, city, township, and county levels. Although most government veterinarians work in public health, the military, or for food inspection programs, they can fill a variety of positions.

For example, most law enforcement agencies (such as the FBI) use dogs for tracking and detection work. Think about the number of dogs used in the aftermath of the World Trade Center disaster. Veterinarians working for the government looked after many of these dogs. Similarly, all animals in the service of different government agencies (including emergency response agencies and the Department of Homeland Security) receive care from government veterinarians.

This dog is searching for contraband.

Two of our largest government agencies, the U.S. Department of Agriculture and the Food and Drug Administration, employ numerous veterinarians at various levels, from directors and administrators to field officers stationed throughout the country.

Animals commonly are an important part of space exploration research, and veterinarians working for the government are of critical importance in this work. In fact, veterinarians have been members of space shuttle crews.

If you are interested in endangered species preservation, you might find a position among the many veterinarians who work for government programs aimed at restoring these species. Veterinary careers in government can include wildlife veterinarians studying grizzly bears and wolves in the Rocky Mountains and exotic animal veterinarians caring for the wide assortment of exotic animals at the National Zoo in Washington, D.C.

NASA astronaut Richard M. Linnehan, DVM, has used his veterinary knowledge in space.

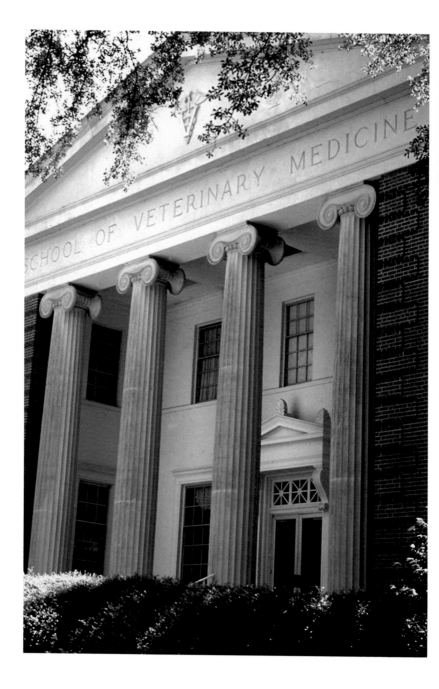

Veterinary Education and Career Development

Many individuals decide to become a veterinarian because they love animals. That is, of course, vitally important. However, a strong interest in science and helping people is just as important.

Because becoming a veterinarian is challenging and takes a lot of work and time, it is best to develop a plan early on that will help you meet the entry requirements of an accredited veterinary college. It is not easy to get into veterinary school, and like most things worth pursuing, it will require much hard work, dedication, and commitment. Think about your plans for earning the Eagle Scout badge. Isn't the same true?

Preparation to become a veterinarian begins today, long before you enter college. Strive to develop academic strength in the biological and physical sciences. Also, develop a well-rounded education by participating in clubs, teams, and other school activities. Along with your Scouting achievements, your extracurricular activities will help admissions committees form a positive picture of you.

Following graduation from high school, you must complete an undergraduate program at a college or university before attending veterinary school. Most students earn a bachelor of science degree before applying to a college of veterinary medicine. Other students earn a master of science or a doctor of philosophy beforehand, although it is not required to do so.

Plan to apply 14 to 18 months before the date you want to enter veterinary school.

The *Veterinary Medical School Admission Requirements in the United States and Canada* provides a complete list of prerequisites required by all of the U.S. and Canadian veterinary colleges accredited by the AVMA.

A doctorate in veterinary medicine requires six to eight years of education after high school.

When you are ready to apply to schools of veterinary medicine, request informational packets from each school in which you are interested. Ask about prerequisite courses and exams, admissions office contacts, application deadlines, advanced-standing policies, combined/dual-degree programs, summer programs, and statistical data from recent applicant pools.

It also is not necessary to receive an undergraduate degree from a university that houses a college of veterinary medicine. In fact, many states do not have a veterinary college. However, you should choose a college or university with strong science programs.

It is not necessary to enroll in "pre-veterinary" or "pre-vet" undergraduate programs, but you must make sure you complete all the prerequisites required by the veterinary medical college you wish to attend. Prerequisites vary from college to college. If you plan to apply to more than one veterinary college, you must meet the requirements for each school. Standardized testing requirements also vary between schools: You might need to take the Graduate Record Examination (GRE) and/or the Medical College Admission Test (MCAT).

Make sure to include time for veterinary experience in your plans. Working or volunteering at veterinary clinics, animal shelters, farms, and ranches will provide many first-hand insights into the career. Be sure to keep a record of your veterinary experiences, including the dates of your involvement and what you learned. This will make your application to veterinary school more attractive to the admission boards.

If there is a veterinary college in your home state, develop a relationship with that school. Most state-supported schools show preference to state residents but do accept a limited number of out-of-state applicants. These positions are highly competitive, however. If you live in a state that does not have a veterinary college, find out if a school in another state has an arrangement for students from your state.

Before you apply, visit at least one veterinary college. Many veterinary colleges hold annual open houses for prospective applicants. This gives applicants the opportunity to tour the school and talk with faculty and students. You might be able to visit a veterinary college while working on this merit badge. Ask your merit badge counselor to help you arrange such a visit.

Once in veterinary school, plan on at least four years of rigorous training. The first two years involve basic classroom study. In the first year, courses cover subjects such as anatomy, physiology (the study of body chemistry), histology (microscopic anatomy), and other subjects about the basic structure of animals. The second year centers on disease mechanisms such as microbiology, parasites, and pathology (how disease affects tissue). In the third year, medical and surgical treatment begins. The fourth year consists of clinical work ranging from cardiology to urology, in-house clinical patients to outpatient farm-call patients, and zoo animals and exotic pets to birds and fish.

After completion of veterinary school, a veterinarian must pass national and state board examinations before he or she can practice veterinary medicine. Some veterinary graduates pursue advanced training in one of over 20 specialties, such as ophthalmology (eye diseases and eye surgery) or orthopedic (bone) surgery.

Pursuing a doctor of veterinary medicine (D.V.M. or V.M.D.) degree might seem like a long road. But just as with earning your Eagle Scout badge, it is well worth the effort. As with many other professional degrees, like dentistry, law, human medicine, and engineering, there is a lot to learn. The trick is to start early and do your best.

Veterinary Technicians

Veterinary technicians are essential members of any veterinary team. Called animal health technicians (A.H.T.) or registered veterinary technicians (R.V.T.), they perform many of the same tasks that nurses perform for physicians.

Veterinary technicians are trained in the care and handling of normal and sick animals and can perform routine laboratory and clinical tests, exams, and procedures. Veterinary technicians must work under the supervision of a licensed veterinarian, and they cannot diagnose, prescribe, or perform surgery on their own. However, they generally assist in all aspects of the medical and surgical care that veterinarians provide.

Though most veterinary technicians work for veterinarians in companion or small animal medicine, many assist in equine and large animal veterinary practices. However, career options

A career as a veterinary technician might be for you if you care about animals, are good at working with your hands, understand the basic sciences, and enjoy working with people while also juggling a changing series of responsibilities.

for veterinary technicians are increasing rapidly. Veterinary technicians can now be found working in biomedical research, schools, zoos, diagnostic laboratories, military and government services, food inspection programs, drug and feed companies, and humane societies and animal shelters. As with most careers, the variety of employment opportunities offers a range of salaries and benefits depending on ability and experience and the responsibilities, assignments, and location of a particular position.

The American Veterinary Medical Association accredits veterinary technician programs throughout the United States. Training to become a veterinary technician usually begins in one of these programs. Most accredited programs lead to an associate's degree after two years of study. However, veterinary technicians with a bachelor of science degree typically earn a higher salary and have more responsibilities. In addition to course work, students of veterinary technician programs complete a certain amount of hands-on training, which is a critical part of all accredited programs. Finally, nearly every state requires that veterinary technicians pass a state and/or national examination to be eligible to practice.

For a complete list of veterinary technology programs, many accredited by the American Veterinary Medical Association, visit the AVMA's website at http://www.avma.org.

The Human-Animal Bond and the Veterinarian

The human-animal bond has existed since humans first asked animals to be their guardians around the cave and campfire, their companions, their hunting partners, and their beasts of burden. Hieroglyphics on the Egyptian pyramids illustrate the human-animal bond, and Roman legends tell about it in stories such as "Romulus and Remus," who were nursed by a wolf. Today, studies show that more than 75 percent of pet owners consider their pets to be members of the family. Further, one third of those pet owners consider their pets to be people.

The human-animal bond does not exist just because a person is in the company of an animal. Rather, it is the bond that develops because of the mutual benefit animals and

The highly enjoyable writings of James Herriot—author of *All Creatures Great and Small*—tell the human side of the human-animal bond.

humans gain from each other. For humans, companionship, security, and a sense of belonging are some of the rewards of bonding with a pet. Having pets gives people a sense of personal responsibility, an opportunity for physical exercise and play, and a perceived need to take better care of themselves, if only for the welfare of the pet. Pets benefit from the care that people provide.

If you have a pet, you know how special that pet is to you. Ask yourself why you feel the way you do about your pet. The answers from your deepest feelings reflect your experience with the human-animal bond. Beyond your day-to-day experience with it, the human-animal bond affects people's lives in subtle yet significant ways. For example, the human-animal bond has been shown to lower blood pressure, shorten recovery time following surgery, reduce stress, and improve self-esteem and emotional well-being.

The veterinarian's role is to recognize and understand the importance of the human-animal bond and to enhance it. Veterinarians can do this by being compassionate advisers for an animal's health-care needs throughout the animal's lifetime. This includes providing quality medical care and giving advice to people about animal care, preventive medical care, and how to choose the right pet.

A Day in the Life of a Veterinarian

With all of the different areas of practice and the different animals and conditions to treat, it is easy to see that a veterinarian's day is never dull. Moreover, there is a lot of overlap between fields. For example, a companion animal veterinarian might see an exotic animal occasionally, or a large animal veterinarian might treat a dog while on a farm call.

In fact, all of the veterinary fields described in this merit badge pamphlet share common ground. For any veterinarian, a day's work might start in the middle of the night and continue until midnight the next evening (emergencies do occur). In addition, veterinarians often travel and work weekends and holidays. All veterinarians promise to work at a certain level of excellence and professional integrity. Within the heart of all veterinarians is a basic compassion for animals and their owners. Lastly, common to all veterinarians is a deep respect for the veterinary profession itself.

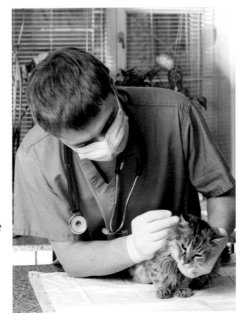

If you decide to pursue a career in veterinary medicine, you are choosing a journey filled with a variety of experiences, limitless professional opportunities, and deep personal satisfaction. This life journey will provide you with the pleasure of knowing that you have made a difference in the lives of both people and animals.

Veterinary Medicine Resources

Scouting Literature

Animal Science, Bird Study, Dog Care, Fish and Wildlife Management, Horsemanship, Mammal Study, Nature, Pets, Public Health, and *Reptile and Amphibian Study* merit badge pamphlets

Visit the Boy Scouts of America's official retail website at http://www.scoutstuff.org for a complete listing of all merit badge pamphlets and other helpful Scouting materials and supplies.

Books

Association of American Veterinary Medical Colleges, et al. *Veterinary Medical School Admission Requirements in the United States and Canada.* Purdue University Press, 2013.

Croke, Vicki, Philip C. Kosch, et al. *Animal ER: Extraordinary Stories of Hope and Healing From One of the World's Leading Veterinary Hospitals.* Plume, 2000.

James Herriot. *All Creatures Great and Small.* St. Martin's Press, 2004.

————. *All Things Bright and Beautiful.* St. Martin's Press, 2004.

Lee, Mary Price, and Richard S. Lee. *Opportunities in Animal and Pet Care Careers,* 2nd ed. McGraw-Hill/Contemporary Books, 2008.

Maynard, Thane, and Jane Goodall. *Working With Wildlife: A Guide to Careers in the Animal World.* Franklin Watts, 1999.

Maze, Stephanie, and Catherine O'Neill Grace. *I Want to Be . . . A Veterinarian.* Harcourt, 1997.

Pavia, Audrey. *Careers With Animals.* Barron's Educational Series, 2001.

Organizations and Websites

American Animal Hospital Association
12575 West Bayaud Ave.
Lakewood, CO 80228-2012
Toll-free telephone: 800-252-2242
Website: http://www.aahanet.org

American Association of Bovine Practitioners
P.O. Box 3610
Auburn, AL 36831-3610
Telephone: 334-821-0442
Website: http://www.aabp.org

American Association of Equine Practitioners
4075 Iron Works Parkway
Lexington, KY 40511
Telephone: 859-233-0147
Website: http://www.aaep.org

American Association of Swine Veterinarians
830 26th Street
Perry, IA 50220-2328
Telephone: 515-465-5255
Website: http://www.aasv.org

American Association of Wildlife Veterinarians
Website: http://www.aawv.net

American Association of Zoo Veterinarians
581705 White Oak Road
Yulee, FL 32097
Telephone: 904-225-3275
Website: http://www.aazv.org

American Veterinary Medical Association
1931 N. Meacham Road, Suite 100
Schaumburg, IL 60173-4360
Telephone: 800-248-2862
Website: http://www.avma.org

Association of Avian Veterinarians
P.O. Box 9
Teaneck, NJ 07666
Telephone: 720-458-4111
Website: http://www.aav.org

Association of Reptilian and Amphibian Veterinarians
810 East 10th Street
P.O. Box 1897
Lawrence, KS 66044-8897
Website: http://www.arav.org

Canadian Veterinary Medical Association
339 Booth St.
Ottawa, Ontario, Canada K1R 7K1
Telephone: 613-236-1162
Website: http://www.canadianveterinarians.net

Veterinary Medical Schools and Colleges in the United States and Canada

ACCREDITED BY THE AMERICAN VETERINARY MEDICAL ASSOCIATION

Auburn University
College of Veterinary Medicine
Auburn, Alabama

Tuskegee University
School of Veterinary Medicine
Tuskegee, Alabama

University of California
School of Veterinary Medicine
Davis, California

Western University of Health Sciences
College of Veterinary Medicine
Pomona, California

Colorado State University
College of Veterinary Medicine
and Biomedical Sciences
Fort Collins, Colorado

University of Florida
College of Veterinary Medicine
Gainesville, Florida

University of Georgia
College of Veterinary Medicine
Athens, Georgia

University of Illinois
College of Veterinary Medicine
Urbana, Illinois

Purdue University
School of Veterinary Medicine
West Lafayette, Indiana

Iowa State University
College of Veterinary Medicine
Ames, Iowa

Kansas State University
College of Veterinary Medicine
Manhattan, Kansas

Louisiana State University
School of Veterinary Medicine
Baton Rouge, Louisiana

Tufts University
School of Veterinary Medicine
North Grafton, Massachusetts

Michigan State University
College of Veterinary Medicine
East Lansing, Michigan

The University of Minnesota
College of Veterinary Medicine
St. Paul, Minnesota

Mississippi State University
College of Veterinary Medicine
Starkville, Mississippi

University of Missouri
College of Veterinary Medicine
Columbia, Missouri

Cornell University
College of Veterinary Medicine
Ithaca, New York

North Carolina State University
College of Veterinary Medicine
Raleigh, North Carolina

The Ohio State University
College of Veterinary Medicine
Columbus, Ohio

Oklahoma State University
College of Veterinary Medicine
Stillwater, Oklahoma

Oregon State University
College of Veterinary Medicine
Corvallis, Oregon

University of Pennsylvania
School of Veterinary Medicine
Philadelphia, Pennsylvania

University of Tennessee
College of Veterinary Medicine
Knoxville, Tennessee

Texas A&M University
College of Veterinary Medicine
College Station, Texas

Virginia Tech and
   University of Maryland
Virginia-Maryland Regional College
   of Veterinary Medicine
Blacksburg, Virginia

Washington State University
College of Veterinary Medicine
Pullman, Washington

The University of Wisconsin-Madison
School of Veterinary Medicine
Madison, Wisconsin

University of Montreal
Faculty of Veterinary Medicine
Saint-Hyacinthe, Quebec, Canada

Ontario Veterinary College
University of Guelph
Guelph, Ontario, Canada

University of Prince Edward Island
Atlantic Veterinary College
Charlottetown, Prince Edward
   Island, Canada

University of Saskatchewan
Western College of Veterinary Medicine
Saskatoon, Saskatchewan, Canada

Acknowledgments

The Boy Scouts of America is grateful to the following individuals for their contribution to this new edition of the *Veterinary Medicine* merit badge pamphlet.

Steve Bowen, D.V.M., companion animal veterinarian, El Centro, California

Tom Catanzaro, D.V.M., professional veterinary consultant, Golden, Colorado

Bart Gledhill, V.M.D., research, teaching, government veterinarian, Alamo, California

Paul Stull, D.V.M., companion animal and exotic animal veterinarian, Dayton, Ohio

The Boy Scouts of America is grateful to the men and women serving on the Merit Badge Maintenance Task Force for the improvements made in updating this pamphlet.

Photo Credits

Jupiterimages—pages 9, 25, and 40 *(bottom)*

NASA, courtesy—page 31 *(bottom)*

©Photos.com—cover *(all except merit badge)*; pages 18 *(prairie dog)*, 19, and 20 *(top)*

Ringling Brothers Barnum and Bailey Circus, courtesy—page 17

Shutterstock.com—page 43 (©Byelikova Oksana/Shutterstock, courtesy)

Thinkstock—pages 36–37

U.S. Department of Agriculture; photo by Scott Bauer—page 30

U.S. Department of Agriculture; photo by Jack Dykinga—page 27

U.S. Department of Agriculture; photo by Ken Hammond—pages 22 and 31 *(top)*

U.S. Department of Agriculture; photo by Larry Rana—page 21 *(bottom)*

U.S. Department of Agriculture, Agricultural Research Service, courtesy—page 21 *(top)*

U.S. Fish and Wildlife Service, courtesy—page 23

University of Georgia at Athens, College of Veterinary Medicine, courtesy—page 32

Wikimedia Commons; photo by Agência Brasil—page 39

All other photos not mentioned above are the property of or are protected by the Boy Scouts of America.

Brian Payne—pages 4, 6 *(top, bottom)*, 8, 11–14 *(all)*, 16 *(both)*, 18 *(top)*, 29, 38, 40 *(top)*, 41, and 42

Steve Seeger—pages 6 *(center)*, 18 *(guinea pig)*, 20 *(bottom)*, 26, and 48

OVERCOMING BARRIERS

What Is Sign Language?

Deborah Kent

Enslow Elementary
an imprint of

Enslow Publishers, Inc.
40 Industrial Road
Box 398
Berkeley Heights, NJ 07922
USA

http://www.enslow.com

Enslow Elementary, an imprint of Enslow Publishers, Inc.

Enslow Elementary® is a registered trademark of Enslow Publishers, Inc.

Copyright © 2012 by Deborah Kent

Library of Congress Cataloging-in-Publication Data

Kent, Deborah.
     What is sign language? / Deborah Kent.
        p. cm. — (Overcoming barriers)
     Includes bibliographical references and index.
     Summary: "Begins with the story of Beanca, a girl who was born deaf and uses American Sign Language (ASL) to communicate, and then goes on to explain the history of ASL"—Provided by publisher.
     ISBN 978-0-7660-3771-7
     1. American Sign Language—Juvenile literature. 2. Deaf—Means of communication—United States—Juvenile literature. I. Title.
     HV2476.K463 2011
     419'.7—dc22

                                  2010019683

Future editions:
Paperback ISBN 978-1-4644-0156-5
ePUB ISBN 978-1-4645-1063-2
PDF ISBN 978-1-4646-1063-9

Printed in the United States of America

012012 The HF Group, North Manchester, IN

10 9 8 7 6 5 4 3 2 1

Photo Credits: Associated Press, pp. 16, 26, 37; Courtesy Claudia Gordon, p. 33 (top); Courtesy of Helene Maram pp. 4, 6, 7, 8, 41, 42; Courtesy Paula Tucker, p. 33 (bottom); Courtesy Trix Bruce, p. 32; Gallaudet University Archives, pp. 23, 24; The Granger Collection, New York, p. 22; iStockphoto.com: © Kim Gunkel, p. 15 (girl); © Loretta Hostettler, pp. 13, 14, 30, 31; Library of Congress, pp. 20, 25; © Michael Newman/PhotoEdit, p. 34; Shutterstock.com, pp. 2, 12, 15 (boy), 18.

Cover Photo: Shutterstock.com

Contents

Beanca Turner was born deaf but can still communicate with the world around her.

Chapter 1

Words in Her Hands

When most children start kindergarten, they already understand about three thousand words. For Beanca Turner, however, learning language was different.

Beanca was born deaf. When her mother and father spoke to her, she was not able to hear anything they said. Since she did not hear spoken language, she did not learn to speak. Sometimes she made up hand gestures to mean words such as EAT, HOUSE, or CAR. These hand movements are called home signs. Home signs helped Beanca express simple things, but she could not ask questions or tell stories. When she felt happy, she could not tell her family why. When she felt sad, she could not explain what was wrong.

At school, Beanca and her classmates learned American Sign Language.

Everything changed for Beanca when she went to school. All the children in her class were deaf. The teacher communicated with the children by forming signs with her hands. The signs were words and ideas that the deaf children could see and understand. The teacher was using American Sign Language (ASL).

Beanca and the other children watched the teacher. They learned new signs every day. Soon Beanca was using these signs to ask questions, tell stories, and explain how she felt. For the first time in her life, Beanca could communicate with other people. She could understand what they said to her.

Beanca began to use ASL with her family. Her mother and father took ASL classes so they could

Beanca's family learned ASL so that they could all communicate.

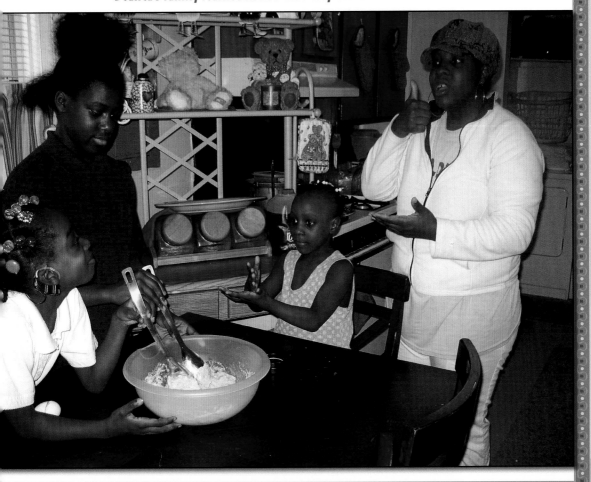

Beanca and her brother sign to each other.

communicate with Beanca. Beanca's older brother and sister learned some signs, too. Her younger sister learned to sign very well. She became the best signer in the family after Beanca herself.

ASL is Beanca's first language. She is learning to read and write English, too. She has written several books with her own stories and pictures. She practices speaking English words every day. She is learning to

Beanca's Favorite Things

Today Beanca is nine years old. She is a fourth grader in Calumet City, Illinois. She uses ASL in all of her classes. Her favorite subjects are art, gym, and math. She loves to draw and make up stories. Beanca also likes to watch TV and play with her sisters. After school she takes care of her pet hamster. She feeds him and cleans his cage. Sometimes she takes him out and lets him go exploring around her room.

understand spoken English by watching people's lips as they talk. This is called lipreading.

When the weather is nice, Beanca and her sisters play outside. Other kids see them signing to each other and don't know what they are saying. Sometimes they stare. Sometimes they ask Beanca's sisters to teach them a few signs. Beanca wishes that more kids would learn ASL. If the kids in her neighborhood knew ASL, it would be easier to make friends.

Chapter 2

What Is American Sign Language?

Talk, talk, talk! Most of us talk from the time we wake up in the morning until we go to bed at night. If you can hear, you usually talk by using your voice. Thousands of spoken languages are used throughout the world. English, Spanish, Korean, and Swahili are just a few of the many, many languages spoken today.

Not all languages use sound and speech. If you are deaf, you usually cannot hear spoken words. Many deaf people all over the world use sign languages. Sign languages are made up of words and concepts that are

Sign languages are used all over the world, but they are not the *same* language. Each country has its own sign language. For example, there is French Sign Language and American Sign Language.

This boy is signing the word "telephone."

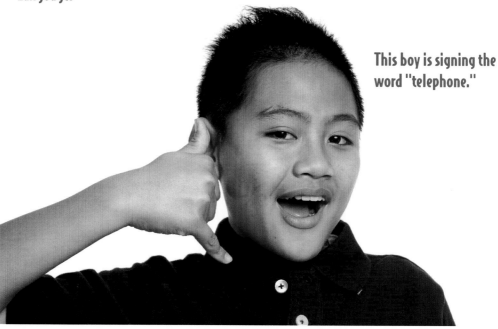

expressed using the hands, face, and body. American Sign Language, or ASL, is the sign language used most widely in the United States and Canada.

ASL is made up of thousands of signs. Some signs stand for objects, such as CHAIR, DOLL, or BIRD. Some signs stand for action words and can be understood easily by non-signers, such as THROW, WALK, or EAT. There are signs for words that describe things, such as BLUE, LONG, DEEP, or PRETTY. Like any other language, ASL also has signs for words that ask questions, such as WHO, WHAT, and WHY.

Every language has its own rules of grammar. For example, in English, people usually put a descriptive word, called an adjective, in front of a word that stands

This woman is signing the word "who."

This woman is signing the word "cat."

The girl is signing the word "father."
The boy is signing the word "mother."

for an object (a noun). We talk about "a blue plate," "a big dog," or "a tall girl." In Spanish, however, the adjective comes after the noun. A blue plate is "un plato azul" and a big dog is "un perro grande."

Like spoken languages, sign languages have their own rules of grammar. The grammar of ASL is very different from the grammar of English. An important

Helen Keller was both deaf and blind. She traveled to many countries working for world peace and for the rights of deaf and blind people. Helen Keller never learned ASL. Instead, she used fingerspelling by touch. To speak with her, a person fingerspelled into her hand. She could "read" fingerspelling with amazing speed.

Helen Keller, left, learned fingerspelling from her teacher, Anne Sullivan. Here, Helen is lipreading.

word might come at the start of a sentence, or be saved for the end to give it more meaning. When Beanca signs, ME CURIOUS WANT KNOW WHAT YOU DOING ALL OF YOU, she means, in English, "I want to know what you are doing, my friends."

Some signs are like pictures drawn with the hands. For instance, to make the sign for SKY, spread your

American Sign Language Alphabet

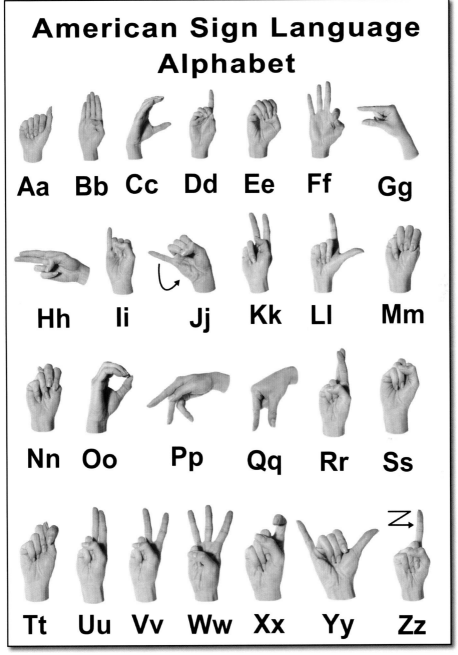

Aa Bb Cc Dd Ee Ff Gg

Hh Ii Jj Kk Ll Mm

Nn Oo Pp Qq Rr Ss

Tt Uu Vv Ww Xx Yy Zz

This chart shows the finger movements for each letter in the American Sign Language alphabet.

ASL uses fingerspelling for people's names. (Fingerspelling is a system for signing the letters of the alphabet to spell names and some words.) However, instead of spelling out the whole name, the signer may use a name sign. A name sign is usually given to a person by another deaf person. It is most often the first letter of the person's name, signed at a certain place on the face or upper body. For example, the letter D formed above the signer's head might be the name sign for a boy named Darrell who is very tall. Sometimes there is no special reason for a name sign except that it is the first letter of a person's name.

palm outward in front of your forehead. Make a sweeping motion with your hand from left to right. To make the sign for CAT, touch your cheek with your thumb and forefinger. Then move your hand outward to show the cat's whiskers.

Most words in ASL are not easy for non-signers to recognize. To make the sign for MOTHER, touch the tip of your thumb to your chin and spread your hand open, fingers pointing upward. The sign for FATHER is the same, but with your thumb touching your forehead.

When people sign in ASL they use their faces and bodies to help carry their meaning. When a boy tells a story he may show fear, surprise, or joy on his face. When a girl is angry, she may sign with sharp, jabbing movements.

Each letter of the alphabet has its own handshape. Signing a word or name letter by letter is called fingerspelling. Sometimes signers fingerspell a word to give it more emphasis. If a signer spells S-T-O-P, it can be like shouting the word. Sometimes a signer may sign the word first and then say it again with fingerspelling, or vice versa.

In general, when two people speak different languages, they may blend the languages together. Sometimes deaf and hearing people use signs from ASL and follow the rules of English grammar. This style of signing is called Pidgin Signed English, or PSE.

Thomas Hopkins Gallaudet was inspired to help deaf children after meeting Alice Cogswell.

Chapter 3

A New Language for a New Nation

One day in 1812, a young man named Thomas Hopkins Gallaudet had dinner with his neighbors, the Cogswells. The Gallaudets and the Cogswells lived in Hartford, Connecticut. After dinner Gallaudet sat with nine-year-old Alice Cogswell. Alice had been deaf since the age of two. Although she had attended school for a short time, she had no way to talk to her family.

Gallaudet showed Alice a hat and wrote the letters H-A-T in the dirt with a stick. At first Alice did not understand what the letters meant. Then all of a sudden the meaning was clear to her. With a big smile

she wrote H-A-T in the dirt and dropped the hat over the letters. She understood that the letters stood for the hat itself.

In 1812, the United States had been a nation for fewer than forty years. It had no schools for deaf children. Gallaudet went to England to learn about methods of teaching deaf children there. The English teachers refused to help him. Gallaudet then went to France to visit a school for the deaf in Paris. Students at the school used French Sign Language as their first language.

Gallaudet spent months at the school. He learned everything he could from the teachers and students. He returned to the United States with one of the

French teachers, a deaf man named Laurent Clerc. Clerc taught French Sign Language to Gallaudet. In turn, Gallaudet taught English to Clerc. He wrote on a slate board, which is like a small blackboard.

In 1817, Gallaudet, Laurent Clerc, and Alice's father, Mason Fitch Cogswell, started a school for deaf children in Hartford. It was the first school for the deaf in the United States. Some of the students came from Martha's Vineyard, an island off the coast of Massachusetts. The island children already knew a sign language, sometimes called Martha's Vinyard Sign Language. They taught their language to the other students at the Hartford school. The children added words and rules of grammar from French Sign Language, which they learned from

CLERC, *Sourd-Muet, Élève de M.ͬ Sicard. Instituteur des Sourds-Muets, aux États-unis.*

Laurent Clerc helped Gallaudet create the first signs in American Sign Language.

Gallaudet and Clerc. They may also have mixed in some of their own home signs. American Sign Language (ASL) grew from these roots. Over the years it became a true language with its own words and rules.

More and more schools for deaf children opened in U.S. cities. ASL was used in most of them. Many of the teachers were deaf men and women who were trained by Clerc. The children lived at the schools, too. The students learned to read and write English as a

Gallaudet opened a school for deaf children in Connecticut.

Some deaf students wanted to go to college. Edward Miner Gallaudet, Thomas Hopkins Gallaudet's son, helped start a college for deaf students with the support of the Deaf community. Gallaudet College (today Gallaudet University) opened in 1864 in Washington, D.C. All of the classes were, and continue to be, held in ASL.

second language. They studied literature, art, mathematics, and many other subjects, just like any other students.

Many hearing teachers thought that deaf children should not learn to sign. They thought that only speech and lipreading should be taught. In 1880, a group of hearing teachers from many countries held a meeting in Milan, Italy. Very few deaf teachers were invited.

The American School for the Deaf celebrated its 185th anniversary in 2002. The wooden hands spell out "ASD 185."

At the meeting in Milan, the teachers decided to ban sign language from schools for the deaf all over the world.

In the years that followed, few deaf teachers were hired to teach deaf children in the United States. Hearing teachers forbade their deaf students to use ASL. If students signed, the teacher smacked their hands. If they signed after being scolded, the teacher might tie their hands behind their backs.

Day after day, deaf children watched their teachers' lips and struggled to speak out loud. ASL did not disappear, however. The moment no teacher was looking, the children eagerly signed to one another. They taught ASL to each new student who arrived at the school. They used ASL on the playgrounds, in the dormitories, and at home. ASL continued outside the classroom.

In 1955, a professor named William Stokoe arrived at Gallaudet University to teach literature. By that time only signs in English word order were used in Gallaudet's classrooms. Away from class, however, the students switched to ASL. Stokoe, who could hear,

Hard of Hearing

Not all people with hearing loss think of themselves as deaf. People whose hearing loss is mild are said to be hard of hearing. Someone who is hard of hearing can usually understand most speech, especially if the room is quiet and people speak clearly.

had never seen ASL before. He realized that ASL was a language, and he asked the students to teach it to him.

The students were amazed by Stokoe's interest. No hearing teacher had ever cared about ASL before. When they saw that Stokoe's interest was real, the students grew excited. They taught him ASL and helped him write a dictionary of the language.

Stokoe proved that ASL was a real language of great value to deaf children and adults. He helped ASL gain the respect of hearing teachers, parents, and others across the United States. For the first time in many years, deaf people felt proud of their language and its history. ASL was no longer a secret. It was accepted, and it once again became a source of joy and pride.

Chapter 4

ASL at Work

Deaf people and people who are hard of hearing work as teachers, mechanics, actors, and scientists. In fact, they work in almost any career you can name. I. King Jordan, a past president of Gallaudet University who is deaf himself, is often quoted as saying, "Deaf people can do anything but hear."

Many deaf people and people who are hard of hearing use ASL interpreters to help them on the job. An interpreter translates into signs everything that is being said in spoken English. The interpreter then speaks what the deaf person says in ASL. An ASL interpreter must be highly skilled and certified. He or she must be able to sign quickly enough to keep up with a fast conversation.

An interpreter signs the minister's sermon.

Angela Earhart is a deaf doctor. She uses an ASL interpreter when she talks to her hearing patients. Sometimes she also sees deaf patients. They are thrilled to have a doctor who uses ASL.

Actress and storyteller Trix Bruce has made ASL a part of her work. Using ASL, she performs one-woman shows for both deaf and hearing people.

Many interpreters are the hearing children of deaf parents, called children of deaf adults (CODAs). Some CODAs are fluent signers because they learned ASL as a first language.

Trix Bruce is a deaf actress and storyteller.

Even people who do not know ASL love to watch her graceful hands and lively face.

Claudia Gordon was born on the island of Jamaica. She became deaf when she was eight years old. She learned ASL when she came to the United States to go to school. She has worked as a lawyer. After Hurricane

Claudia Gordon helps make sure that deaf people are treated equally at work.

Katrina struck New Orleans in 2005, Gordon worked to make sure the city's deaf people got the help they needed. She worked to protect the rights of deaf people and people with disabilities during the emergency. She now works for the U.S. Department of Labor.

Christian Vogler is a deaf scientist working at Gallaudet University. He leads a group working on new Internet and communications technology for deaf and hard of hearing people.

Christian Vogler works on creating computer programs that understand ASL.

The boy on the left has a cochlear implant, and the other two boys have different kinds of hearing aids.

Chapter 5

ASL in the Future

A language is far more than a collection of words and rules. The words can make people laugh or cry. A language lets people tell about the things that matter most to them. For people who sign, ASL is rich with meaning. In ASL they tell stories, play games, propose marriage, and mourn lost friends.

Today many deaf people worry that ASL will soon disappear. In the past, deaf children learned ASL from their classmates at schools for the deaf. More and more deaf children today are being placed into public schools with hearing students. There may be only one deaf child in a school full of hearing children. In this case, the deaf child does not have a chance to learn ASL from other deaf children and adults.

Many deaf children can now get a device called a cochlear implant. The implant is a tiny electronic device that a doctor places beneath the skin behind a person's ear. The person wears a small microphone that sends sound to the device. The device sends the sound to the person's auditory nerve. The auditory nerve is the nerve that carries sound to the brain in order for the person to hear. The cochlear implant is sometimes called a bionic ear.

Although it is an important medical advancement, a cochlear implant is not a cure for deafness. When the person removes the microphone he or she is still deaf. Even when someone wears the microphone and uses the implant, it does not give him or her normal hearing. A child who gets an implant must work hard to learn to understand speech. After years of training, a child with an implant may learn to speak clearly.

Deaf people who use ASL are finding ways to teach the language to today's deaf children. Sometimes

As President Obama gives a speech, an interpreter translates the speech into ASL.

Today about half a million people in the United States use ASL as their first language. As many as 2 million people know some ASL. ASL is commonly said to be the fourth most widely used language in the country, after English, Spanish, and French.

they start clubs for deaf children that meet after school and on Saturdays. Deaf children quickly learn to sign when they are in a group with other deaf people who sign. Deaf adults also teach ASL classes for the hearing parents and families of deaf children. They encourage hearing parents to sign with their deaf children at home.

The Americans With Disabilities Act became a law in 1990. It made ASL more available to deaf people in the United States. Some theaters and arenas now hire ASL interpreters to sign during plays and concerts. ASL interpreters also sign during important speeches by the president of the United States and other officials. Hospitals and courtrooms provide ASL interpreters when people ask for them. More hearing people have become interested in learning to sign. Some high schools and colleges now let students study ASL as a foreign language.

Some teachers of deaf children used to fear that a child who used ASL would never learn to speak or lipread. Today many teachers realize that deaf children learn best when they have ASL as their first language. ASL can even help children who have cochlear implants. ASL provides a way to communicate between the time a child gets the implant and the time he or she can begin to make sense of language with the implant. It allows the child to communicate more easily when he or she is not wearing the implant. Also, a child who has mastered one language can more easily learn another.

Chapter 6

Looking Ahead

Over the years, Beanca Turner has had several deaf teachers. They encourage her to think about what she would like to do when she grows up.

Sometimes other deaf people visit Beanca's class and talk to the children. One day Beanca met a deaf mechanic who repairs the engines of airplanes. Once a deaf artist came and talked about his work. Another time Beanca's class had a visit from a deaf photographer. He came from Nigeria in Africa.

Beanca loves to draw and to write stories. She says she would like to be an artist or a writer someday. She also loves to read and thinks she might like to work in a library. Beanca's teacher says she is a very bright

Beanca loves art and writing.

The author of this book, Deborah Kent, visits Beanca at her school.

girl, and she will do whatever she makes up her mind to do.

Beanca now has a cochlear implant. When she uses the implant she has some hearing, and she is learning to speak and lipread. However, when she gets an idea, her thoughts flash from her hands in eager signs. When she is excited or angry or sad, she shares her feelings through sign language. ASL will always be Beanca's first language.

Many thousands of people use ASL when they solve problems or make plans. They sign when they tell jokes or share good news. Throughout their lives they celebrate the ease and beauty of signing.

Words to Know

adjective—A word that describes something.

American Sign Language (ASL)—A language made up of handshapes, body movements, and facial expressions, used by deaf people in the United States and Canada.

auditory nerve—The nerve that carries sound from the ear to the brain so that a person can hear.

cochlear implant—An electronic device that is placed under the skin behind the ear to improve hearing in a deaf person.

fingerspelling—A system for signing the letters of the alphabet, used for spelling names and some words.

fluent—Able to use a language with flowing ease.

grammar—A system of rules about how words are used. These rules help give a language its meaning.

home sign—A gesture invented by a deaf person or his or her family to mean a simple word or idea.

lipreading—A method of understanding spoken language by watching the movements of the speaker's lips, face, and tongue.

noun—A word that stands for a person or object.

Pidgin Signed English—A combination of ASL and English most frequently used by people whose first language is spoken English.

Learn More

Books

Heller, Lora. *Sign Language for Kids: A Fun and Easy Guide to American Sign Language.* New York: Sterling, 2004.

Kent, Deborah. *American Sign Language.* New York: Franklin Watts, 2003.

Kramer, Jackie. *You Can Learn Sign Language!* New York: Scholastic, 2004.

McCully, Emily Arnold. *My Heart Glow: Alice Cogswell, Thomas Gallaudet, and the Birth of American Sign Language.* New York: Hyperion Books for Children, 2008.

Warner, Penny. *Learn to Sign the Fun Way: Let Your Fingers Do the Talking with Games, Puzzles, and Activities in American Sign Language.* Roseville, Calif.: Prima Publishing, 2001.

Web Sites

42 Explore
<http://www.42explore.com/signlang.htm>
Gives basic information about American Sign Language and lists a variety of online resources.

ASL Alphabet Coloring Pages
<http://www.dltk-teach.com/alphabuddies/asl>
Printable pages for each letter of the fingerspelled alphabet.

ASL Info
<http://www.aslinfo.com>
Information and resources on ASL and Deaf culture.

Index